FUN WITH CROSSWORD PUZZLES
Coloring Book

Anna Pomaska

Dover Publications, Inc.
New York

Published in Canada by General Publishing Company, Ltd., 30 Lesmill Road,
Don Mills, Toronto, Ontario.
Published in the United Kingdom by Constable and Company, Ltd., 10
Orange Street, London, WC2H 7EG.

Fun with Crossword Puzzles Coloring Book is a new work, first published by
Dover Publications, Inc., in 1985.

International Standard Book Number: 0-486-24978-6

Manufactured in the United States of America
Dover Publications, Inc., 31 East 2nd Street, Mineola, N.Y. 11501

Publisher's Note

If you can spell, you can do a crossword puzzle, even if you have never done one before. The 21 puzzles in this book are arranged according to the letters of the alphabet. All the words in the first puzzle begin with the letter "A," in the second puzzle with "B," and so on (a few puzzles combine letters: "J" and "K," for example). To begin, look at the pictures on the left-hand page. They should all remind you of familiar things. The words for these things all begin with the main letter of that puzzle. Write these words in the proper boxes.

Let us take the "A" puzzle as an example. The word for the object next to number 1 in the "across" column should be written in the series of five boxes that begins with the number 1 on the puzzle page and goes *across* (from left to right). The word for the object next to number 1 in the "down" column will of course also begin with "A." The "A" will already be written in the box with number 1 in the puzzle, since you began the "across" word with it. Write in the rest of the "down" word, one letter to a box, going *down* (from top to bottom).

You will notice that in all of these puzzles many letters are in two words at the same time. Again using the "A" puzzle as an example, you can see that the eighth letter of the "4 across" word is also the third letter of the "5 down" word. If you do not know the "5 down" word at first, but you do know the third letter (from the "4 across" word) and also the first letter (it has to be an "A" in this puzzle), you will have two clues to the spelling of the word in the "5 down" boxes. This use of a single letter to form a part of two different words at the same time is what makes a word puzzle a *cross*word puzzle.

You will find the solutions to all of the puzzles in the section of this book that begins on page 46. But don't look until you have done your best to solve the puzzles on your own!

Also, don't forget that this puzzle book is also a coloring book. You can have fun coloring the pictures any way you wish, either while you are working on the puzzles or after you have completed them.

 CROSSWORD PUZZLE

ALL THESE PICTURES BEGIN WITH THE LETTER "A"

ACROSS	DOWN
1.	1.
2.	4.
3.	5.
4.	6.
6.	7.

A

1. APPLE
2. ARK
3. ARTIST
4. ALLIGATOR
5. ACORN
6. ARROW
7. ANCHOR

AIRPLANE

APRON

 CROSSWORD PUZZLE

ALL THESE PICTURES BEGIN WITH THE LETTER "B"

ACROSS

②

④

⑤

⑥

DOWN

①.

②.

③.

④.

⑤. ABC

6

B

1. BEAR
2. BEAR
3. BALLOON
4. BALLOON
   BIRD
5. BAT
   BOOK
6. BOX

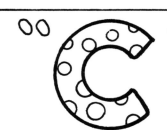 **C** CROSSWORD PUZZLE

ALL THESE PICTURES BEGIN WITH THE LETTER "C"

ACROSS	DOWN

ACROSS

 2.

 3.

6.

 7.

DOWN

1.

 2.

 3.

4.

5.

9

 CROSSWORD PUZZLE

ALL THESE PICTURES BEGIN WITH THE LETTER "D"

ACROSS	DOWN

ACROSS

2.

3.

4.

5.

DOWN

1.

2.

3.

4.

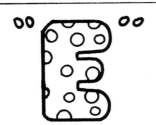 CROSSWORD PUZZLE

ALL THESE PICTURES BEGIN WITH THE LETTER "E"

ACROSS	DOWN

1.

2.

6.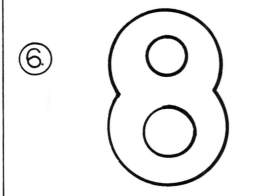

1.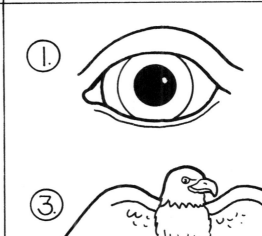

3.

4.

5.

13

 # CROSSWORD PUZZLE

ALL THESE PICTURES BEGIN WITH THE LETTER "F"

ACROSS

 1.

2.

 4.

5.

6.

DOWN

1.

2.

3.

4.

15

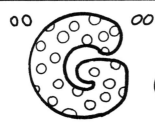 # CROSSWORD PUZZLE

ALL THESE PICTURES BEGIN WITH THE LETTER "G"

ACROSS	DOWN

1.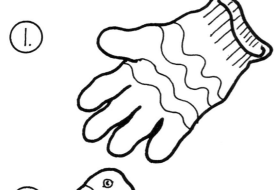

5.

2.

3.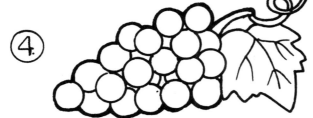

4.

6.

7.

17

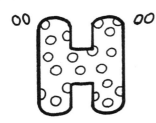 CROSSWORD PUZZLE

ALL THESE PICTURES BEGIN WITH THE LETTER "H"

ACROSS	DOWN

ACROSS

1.

2.

4.

5.

DOWN

1.

2.

3.

5.

19

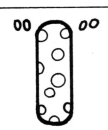

CROSSWORD PUZZLE

ALL THESE PICTURES BEGIN WITH THE LETTER "I"

ACROSS	DOWN

 1.

2.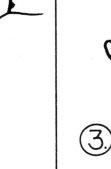

 4.

5.

1.

3.

4.

20

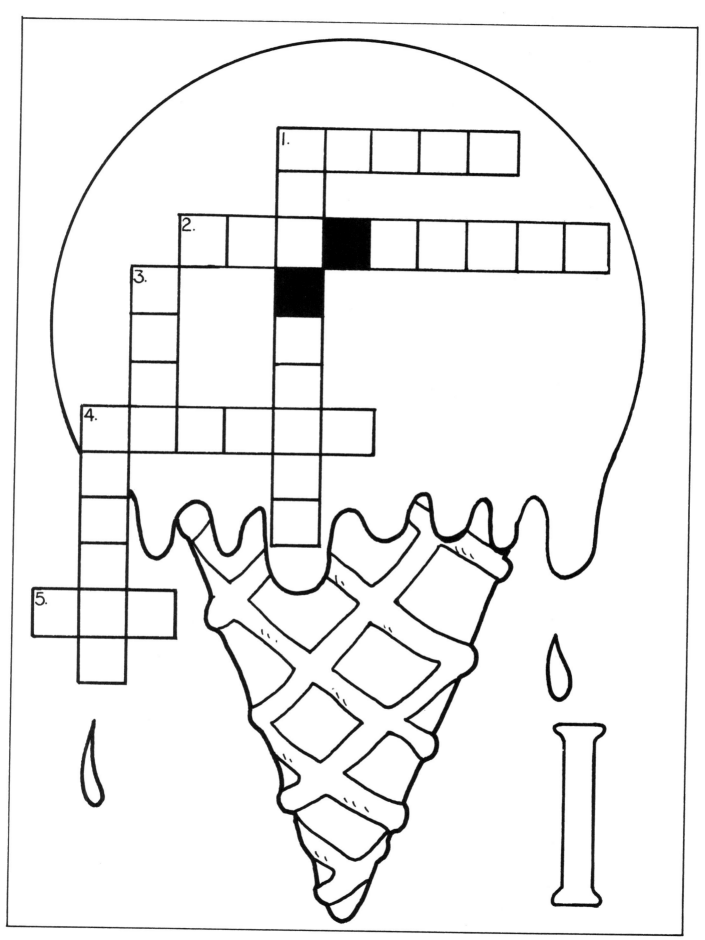

 CROSSWORD PUZZLE

ALL THESE PICTURES BEGIN WITH THE LETTER "J" OR "K"

ACROSS	DOWN

ACROSS

1.

2.

3. GRAPE J

4.

DOWN

5.

6.

7.

8.

 CROSSWORD PUZZLE

ALL THESE PICTURES BEGIN WITH THE LETTER "L"

ACROSS	DOWN

ACROSS

1.

2.

3.

4.

DOWN

1.

2.

4.

5.

24

1. LIPS
   LIZARD
2. LADYBUG
   LEMON
3. LAMP
5. LAMB
4. LION
   LEAF

 CROSSWORD PUZZLE

ALL THESE PICTURES BEGIN WITH THE LETTER "M"

ACROSS	DOWN

ACROSS

1.

2.

3.

4.

5.

DOWN

3.

6.

7.

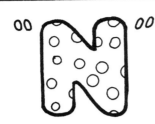 CROSSWORD PUZZLE

ALL THESE PICTURES BEGIN WITH THE LETTER "N"

ACROSS	DOWN

ACROSS

1.

2.

3.

4.

DOWN

1.

2.

3.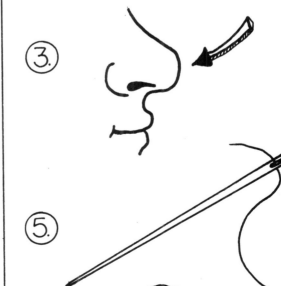

5. (image)

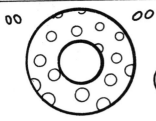

CROSSWORD PUZZLE

ALL THESE PICTURES BEGIN WITH THE LETTER "o"

ACROSS	DOWN
1.	1.
2.	2.
3.	
4.	3.

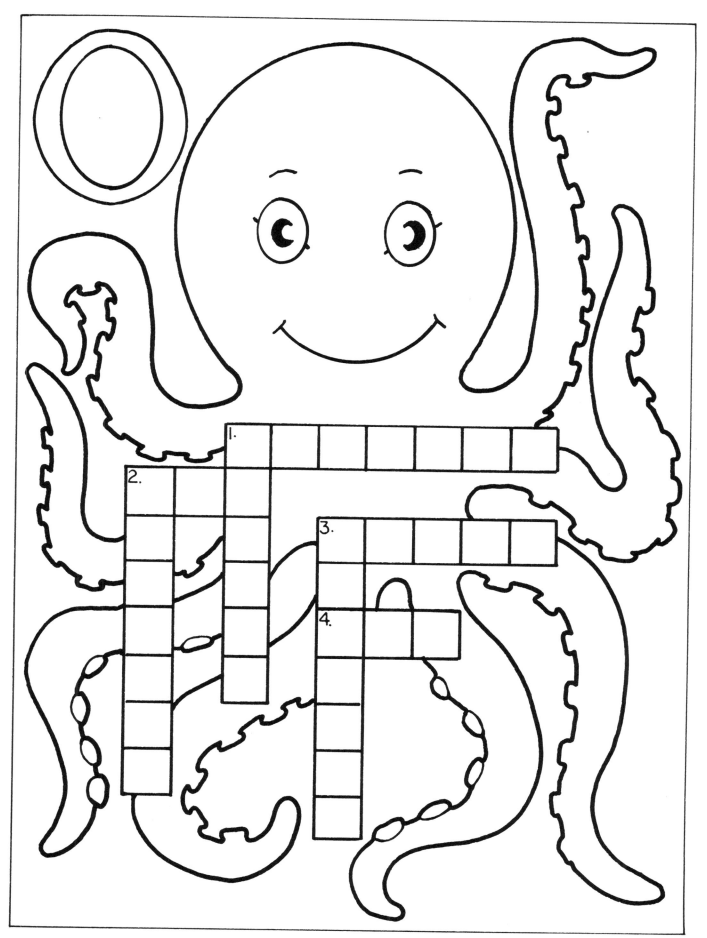

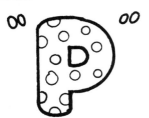 # CROSSWORD PUZZLE

ALL THESE PICTURES BEGIN WITH THE LETTER "P"

ACROSS	DOWN
1.	2.
2.	3.
3.	6.
4.	7.
5.	

32

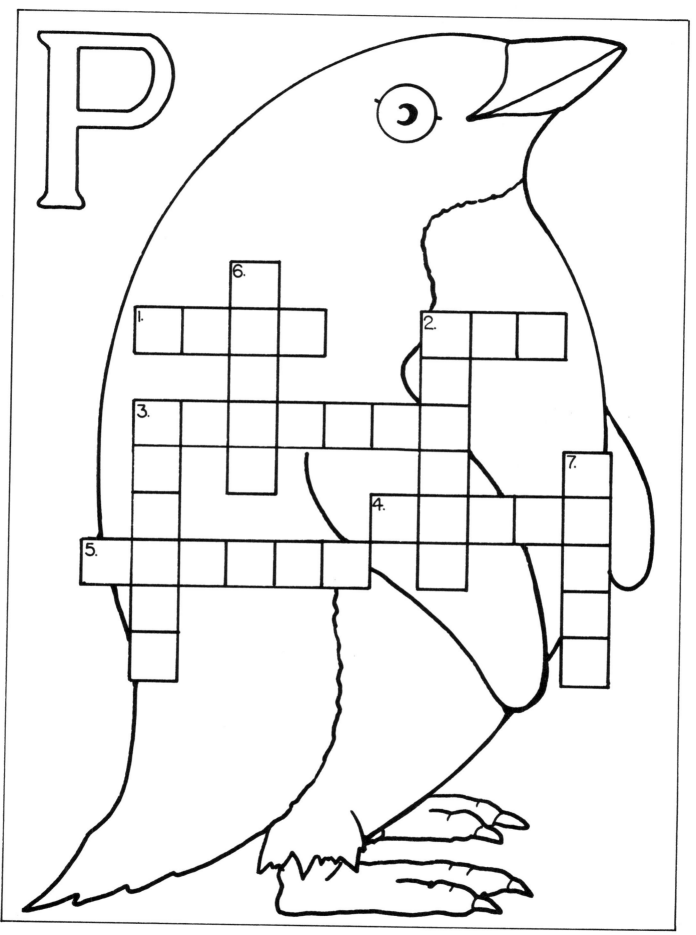

P

33

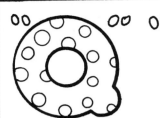  CROSSWORD PUZZLE

ALL THESE PICTURES BEGIN WITH THE LETTER "Q" OR "R"

ACROSS	DOWN
1.	1.
2.	2.
3.	3.
4.	4.

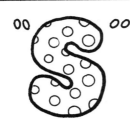 **CROSSWORD PUZZLE**

ALL THESE PICTURES BEGIN WITH THE LETTER "S"

ACROSS	DOWN
2.	1.
4.	2.
5.	3.
6.	6.

CROSSWORD PUZZLE

ALL THESE PICTURES BEGIN WITH THE LETTER "T"

ACROSS	DOWN
1.	1.
3.	2.
4.	4.
5.	6.
7.	

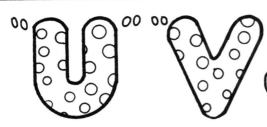 CROSSWORD PUZZLE

ALL THESE PICTURES BEGIN WITH THE LETTER "U" or "V"

ACROSS

1.
2.
3.
4.

DOWN

1.
2.
3.
5.

BE MINE

1.
2.
3.
4.
5.

U V

41

 CROSSWORD PUZZLE

ALL THESE PICTURES BEGIN WITH THE LETTER "W"

ACROSS	DOWN
1.	1.
2.	2.
3.	3.
4.	5.
	6.

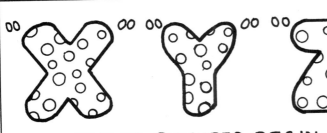 CROSSWORD PUZZLE

ALL THESE PICTURES BEGIN WITH THE LETTER "X," "Y" or "Z"